First Facts®

Staying Safe

Staying Safe Online

by Sally Lee

CAPSTONE PRESS
a capstone imprint

First Facts is published by Capstone Press,
1710 Roe Crest Drive, North Mankato, Minnesota 56003.
www.capstonepub.com

 Books published by Capstone Press are manufactured with paper
containing at least 10 percent post-consumer waste.

Library of Congress Cataloging-in-Publication Data
Lee, Sally.
Staying safe online / by Sally Lee.
    p. cm. — (First facts. staying safe)
  Includes bibliographical references and index.
  Summary: "Discusses the rules and techniques for online safety"—Provided by publisher.
  ISBN 978-1-4296-7617-5 (library binding) — ISBN 978-1-4296-7959-6 (paperback)
  1. Internet—Safety measures—Juvenile literature. I. Title.
  TK5105.875.I57L3925 2012
  364.16'8—dc23   2011021528

Editorial Credits
Christine Peterson, editor; Bobbie Nuytten, designer; Sarah Schuette, photo stylist; Marcy Morin,
    studio scheduler; Kathy McColley, production specialist

Photo Credits
Capstone Studio/Karon Dubke, cover (main), 1, 5, 6, 7, 8, 10, 13, 17 (both), 18, 20
Shutterstock: Ilya D. Gridnev, cover inset (monkey, right), Jon Kroninger, cover inset (polar bear,
    top), Lukich, cover inset (lion), martellostudio, cover inset (rhino), vblinov, cover inset
    (monkey, left), Veronika Vasilyuk, cover inset (polar bear, bottom)

Essential content terms are **bold** and are defined at the bottom of the spread where
they first appear.

Printed in the United States of America in North Mankato, Minnesota.
102011   006405CGS12

Table of Contents

The Internet

How can you connect your computer to the world? Get on the Internet. You can send messages and learn new things. You can play games and listen to music. Enjoy the Internet, but use it safely.

Internet—a system that allows people to share information with others through computers

Helpful Adults

Trusted adults can help you have fun and stay safe online. Have a trusted adult check your computer's security settings. He or she can make sure the computer blocks unsafe material.

Get an adult's permission before going online. Share your passwords and online activities with a trusted adult. Tell him or her if you see or get something online that makes you feel uncomfortable.

online—using a computer while it is connected to the Internet

password—a word or phrase needed to enter some Internet sites

Personal Information

You don't talk to strangers in public. Follow the same rule on the Internet. When you're online, never share personal information with others. Keep your name, address, phone number, and age private. Ask your friends not to share your personal information with others.

E-mail is a great way to stay in touch with family and friends. Check with a trusted adult before sharing your e-mail address. Never open messages from senders you don't know.

Always check with an adult before opening e-mail **attachments**. Some attachments might hurt your computer. Other attachments may be inappropriate for kids.

attachment—a picture or file sent as part of an e-mail
inappropriate—not right for a certain age group, place, or time

Web Sites

Do you like learning new things? The Internet has millions of Web sites full of information. A search engine finds the sites you need. With an adult's help, find search engines that are safe for kids. Don't sign up for free gifts or contests without an adult's permission.

search engine—a computer program that searches the Internet for information

Welcome

 Add Friends

 Add Photo

 Search Games

 Mobile Lookup

 Messages

 BUG someone!

 Report Unusual Behavior!

10 minutes ago

Angela S.
Has anyone heard of the new Selena Gomez movie coming out? I ♡ SG!

Simon L.
No I haven't, but I hope it's soon! CAN'T WAIT!
I ♡ SG too!

5:34 pm

Leila P.
got SOOOO much homework for this weekend

Malik R.
Sorry L, lets study together and then go to the mall tomorrow night!!!!!

Andrew L.
I can help too - but I can't go anywhere till I clean my room

4:23 pm

Leila P.  > **Andrew L.**

Malik R.
SPIDERS! YUCK!
Leila P.
just kidding - are you scared of spiders?!!!! :)
Andrew L.
nope, i love them...

4:17 pm

Allie N.
⊙ my mom just said i could have my birthday party at th

Social Networks

Online social networks are like clubs. You can chat and play games. Have your parents help you find a safe network for kids your age. Choose friends you already know to be in your network. Never give out personal information or send pictures to people you don't know.

social network—a Web site in which multiple users can share information with others

Chat Rooms

Chat rooms are sites where you can talk to other kids online. But be careful. You never know who you are really chatting with. An adult user could be pretending to be a child. Always ask permission before entering a chat room. Only use chat rooms that are set up for kids. Use a screen name and never share pictures with people you meet online.

chat room—a place online where people exchange computer messages
screen name—a made-up name to use online

Online Bullies

Have you ever come across an online bully? Bullies hurt people through e-mails or online posts. They say mean things or spread lies. Some use threats to scare others. But you can help stop online bullies. Never reply to or share messages from a bully. Show the messages to a trusted adult, and ask him or her for help.

Strangers

The Internet is like the mall. It's full of strangers. Most strangers are nice, but some are not. On the Internet, strangers may pose as kids. They may try to trick kids into meeting them in person. Never tell anyone online who you are or where you live. Never agree to meet someone that you met online.

Hands On:
Make a Safety Pledge

It is important to know the rules when you are using the Internet. Making a written pledge with a trusted adult can help.

What You Need

parent or other trusted adult
pen
paper

What You Do

1. Discuss Internet rules with a parent or trusted adult. Here are some things you can talk about:
   - amount of time allowed on the Internet each day
   - online activities that need an adult's permission
   - personal information that should be kept private
   - Web sites to avoid or that should be blocked
2. Write down the rules on a piece paper.
3. Sign your name at the bottom of the pledge. Have a parent or trusted adult sign too.
4. Keep your signed pledge near your computer to remind you of the rules.

Remember, a pledge is a promise. When you sign this pledge, you are promising to follow the rules.

Glossary

attachment (uh-TACH-muhnt)—a picture or file sent as part of an e-mail

chat room (CHAT ROOM)—a place online where people exchange computer messages

inappropriate (in-uh-PROH-pree-it)—not right for a certain age group, place, or time

Internet (IN-tur-net)—a system that allows people to share information with others through computers

online (on-LINE)—using a computer while it is connected to the Internet

password (PASS-wurd)—a word or phrase needed to enter some Internet sites

screen name (SKREEN NAYM)—a made-up name to use online

search engine (SURCH EN-juhn)—a computer program that searches the Internet for information

social network (SOH-shuhl NET-wurk)—a Web site in which multiple users can share information with others

trusted adult (TRUHS-tud uh-DUHLT)—a grown-up you know who is honest and reliable

Read More

Fields, Jan. *You Can Write Great Letters and E-mails.* You Can Write. Mankato, Minn.: Capstone Press, 2012.

Jakubiak, David J. *A Smart Kid's Guide to Internet Privacy.* Kids Online. New York: PowerKids Press, 2010.

Oxlade, Chris. *My First Internet Guide.* My First Computer Guides. Chicago: Heinemann Library, 2007.

Internet Sites

FactHound offers a safe, fun way to find Internet sites related to this book. All of the sites on FactHound have been researched by our staff.

Here's all you do:

Visit *www.facthound.com*

Type in this code: 9781429676175

Check out projects, games and lots more at
www.capstonekids.com

Index